DRINKING FROM OUR WELL

Foundations for the Ministry of Christian Education in the African Methodist Episcopal Church

A Statement of the
Department of Christian Education

Rev. Kenneth H. Hill, Ph.D.

The colorful background pattern on this book cover is an indigo-dyed Kinte cloth from Ghana. In addition to clothing, African textiles may be used as grave cloths, wall hangings, masquerade costumes, and bed covers.

Plate used by permission from the book:
 African Textiles by Christopher Spring
 Crown Publishers, Inc.
 Cover design and illustration: Sheila R. Williams
 ISBN 0-9633114-0-9

Drinking From Our Well

Second Printing
Copyright © 1992
by the Christian Education Department
African Methodist Episcopal Church.

All rights reserved.
Printed in the United States of America.

Not part of this book may be reproduced in any manner whatsoever without written permission except in the case of brief quotations embodied in critical articles or reviews.

For information, address the Christian Education Department, A.M.E. Church, P.O. Box 24390, Nashville, TN 37202.

"Dr. Hill reminds us with fresh insight, what we are doing, why, and that we can do a new thing. He also leaves us knowing that drinking from our own well is a source of great spiritual renewal."

—Bishop John R. Bryant

CONTENTS

Dedication — vii
Acknowledgments — ix
Preface — xi
Introduction — xiii
Historical Sketch — xv

PART I
THE CHALLENGE OF CHRISTIAN EDUCATION — 1
by Kenneth H. Hill

PART II
CONTEXT OF CHRISTIAN EDUCATION: CHRISTIAN EDUCATION ADMINISTRATION
by Kenneth H. Hill

- Chapter 1 Understanding Christian Education In The African Methodist Episcopal Church — 7
- Chapter 2 Meaning of Curriculum In The African Methodist Episcopal Church — 15
- Chapter 3 Learning, Organizing and Planning Christian Education In The African Methodist Episcopal Church — 19

PART III
CONTENT OF CHRISTIAN EDUCATION: FOUNDATIONS FOR CHRISTIAN EDUCATION

- Chapter 4 Christian Education In The African Methodist Episcopal Church: Some Foundational Principles — 27
  by Louis-Charles Harvey
- Chapter 5 God Our Father, Christ Our Redeemer, Man Our Brother: A Theological Interpretation of The African Methodist Episcopal Church — 31
  by James Cone

Notes — 43
Bibliography — 44

DEDICATION

To my parents, Hughes D. Hill and Dorothy M. Hill, my first teachers of Christian Education, I express infinite thanksgiving for their nurturing.

To my children, Kamasi C. Hill and Nonzwakazi T. Hill, to whom I have attempted to model a Christian life, I express my love.

To my fellow educators, ministers, bishops and lay friends who labor to teach and live out the mission of the African Methodist Episcopal Church, I express my gratitude.

ACKNOWLEDGMENTS

Special thanks to James Cone for permission to reprint his article and Louis Charles-Harvey for his contribution.

To all the good people of African Methodism who gave valuable feedback as I shared some of this material in numerous lectures, seminars and workshops.

PREFACE

"Drink waters out of thine own cistern, and running waters out of thine own well."

PROVERBS 5:15, KJV

Drinking From Our Well is an articulation of the Christ-encounter experienced by African Methodist Christians in the struggle to claim our identity as sons and daughters of Allen. The image of a well is used because spirituality is indeed like living water that springs up from the depths of our faith experiences.

Our experience as Blacks begins with a profound encounter with God and God's will. Character formation takes place within the context of the community. Christian educators share the common task of shaping religious identity. One of the most important skills in character formation is the ability to discern from which wells we drink. From what well will our spirituality, our character, our religious identity be nourished? From which well do we drink as African Methodists? As A.M.E.s our identity has become uncertain, we are tempted to look to others to find answers to our present concerns.

Many of us run around drinking water from countless wells: the well of neo-pentecostalism, biblical fundamentalism, secular humanism and rugged individualism. A vibrant spirituality the African Methodist Episcopal Church can exist only when it sends us back to our roots. We must drink from our own wells.

As a Christian educator, I find myself spending more and more time guiding people to their wells, sharing as best I can the great nourishment which I have found.

We must re-acquire a thirst for the water in our own well, and drink that water in order to become clearer about who we are, and what we have to offer the world.

As A.M.E.s we hold that tradition is the primary well from which we draw in shaping our foundations for Christian education. In this booklet we draw from the well of tradition to illumine the picture and practice of Christian education. It is no longer possible for us to assume a firm foundation of theological understanding among members.

One of the most important tasks before our church today is the establishment of a vital teaching ministry at every level of church life. Rediscovering and recovering our tradition is an important initiation aspect into our story.

Here we reflect together the church's historical, as well as its present, practice of Christian education. Our cloud of witnesses to the A.M.E. story includes the lives of spiritual exemplars of the faith, catechisms, doctrines, rituals, liturgies, writings, prayers, creeds and histories.

As African Methodists see more clearly who we have been. As we learn more effectively how to use our heritage, we will become more able to fulfill our calling and discern who we may become. It is in this spirit that we seek to engage in a ministry of Christian education that serves both the diversity and unity of African Methodists.

Rev. Kenneth H. Hill, Ph.D.

INTRODUCTION

"It is our aim that we shall spend our 200th anniversary walking into a teaching ministry grounded in the scriptures; ethical responsibility that will turn our families and our nation in new directions; a sharing of opportunity and information; a Proclamation Mission speaking to and witnessing to a reigning Lord. We must walk the paths of history to find new highways to achieving ethical goals and the King of God."

—BISHOP FRANK M. REID, JR.

As A.M.E.s we have our own way of doing Christian education. What is this way? From what sources does our educational ministry spring? What are the various ways by which our people become Christian? What theological foundations support our journey of faith? Toward what ends is our educational ministry directed? What principles guide our planning for the church school and for curriculum resources?

The Book of Discipline charges the Department of Christian education with responsibility for "developing standards, preparing programs, offering classes, teaching Christian education, publishing materials, training people for pastoral ministry and other church vocations" in accordance with the tradition and doctrine of the African Methodist Episcopal Church (159-160, A-K; 170-171, A).

In each congregation there is to be a church school for the purpose of accomplishing the church's educational ministry in accordance with the mission of the church. This booklet is addressed to all who plan for

Christian education at whatever level of the church, all who administer its varied work, all who teach, all who train leaders or prepare resources.

This booklet is a statement of the challenge, context and content of Christian education in the A.M.E. Church. To ensure that the Christian Education Department's work is theologically grounded, we sought out some of African Methodist's outstanding educators.

We asked them to reflect on Christian education in the light of scripture, tradition and doctrine of our denomination. The following writings by A.M.E. educators offers fresh insights on the nature of Christian education.

This booklet is divided into three parts. Part one relates our tradition to our present situation and challenges us to reclaim a broader understanding of Christian education, based on drinking from our own well. Part two explores the connectional shape and form that our education takes. Part three examines our theological foundations.

While not a defintive statement of the foundations of Christian education in the African Methodist Episcopal Church, this document should be viewed as a call to join in forming and formulating the foundations of Christian education. Therefore, we see future editions of this statement reflecting the thinking of the church for that time and situation.

Will you join in this journey?

HISTORICAL SKETCH

The idea of Christian education is deeply rooted in the traditions and history of African Methodism. Christian education in the form of Sunday school work was organized in 1794. Richard Allen, founder and first bishop of the African Methodist Episcopal Church organized the first African American Sunday school at Mother Bethel, Philadelphia.

A formal plan for a Sunday School Union did not develop until 1884 when the General Conference adopted it and elected Charles S. Smith M.D., its corresponding secretary. Rev. Smith was the first African-American Christian education Executive.

Christian education in the form of higher education was established by Rev. Daniel A. Payne, bishop and founder of Wilberforce University in 1856. Rev. Payne is called the Apostle of education in the A.M.E. Church.

Christian education in the form of youth fellowship was organized by Rev. B. W. Arnett in 1900, the Christian Endeavor Society. In 1904 the name became the Allen Christian Endeavor League lead by Rev. Gregg, lead by Dr. J. C. Caldwell in 1908 and Rev. S. S. Morris in 1920.

Christian education in the form of a connectional department was established at the 1936 General Conference and elected Rev. Solmon S. Morris, Sr., to serve as its first General Secretary. The new Christian education department now combined the functions of the Sunday School Union and Allen Christian Endeavor.

Under the leadership and direction of Dr. S. S. Morris, Sr., the Richard Allen Youth Council experienced rapid growth among youth leaders and workers. Dr. Morris served as General Secretary until 1956.

Dr. Andrew White, who served as assistant to Dr. Morris, became General Secretary in 1956. Dr. White's writings on the tradition and heritage of African Methodism expanded significantly, printed curriculum resources of our Zion. Dr. White held office until 1980.

Dr. Edgar L. Mack, became General Secretary in 1980. Dr. Mack's passion for ecumenism lead him to strengthen interdenominational relationships and to build enduring church partnerships. Dr. Mack, held office until his death in 1991.

PART I

The Challenge of Christian Education

The Challenge of Christian Education

There has been a vast reluctance in the church to "recognize varieties of gifts." God calls not only preachers for the ministry, but teachers as well. Unfortunately Black churches have not given due recognition to the importance of teachers of the Word. Preaching, rather than the teaching ministry, has enjoyed widespread popularity within the church.

More attention needs to be given to elevate the educational ministry of the church. Even in instances where Christian education is a ministry, the typical experience has been that education is segmented from the total life of the church into a church, school, and fellowship program.

Christian education must be united with a wholistic understanding of the ministry of the church. It is an essential ministry for interpreting God's liberating word in our times. Whenever the teaching ministry has been neglected, the church has suffered.

One of the great opportunities of the church is to strengthen Christian education. In order for it to become a powerful expression of Christian mission in the future of the A.M.E. Church, attention must be given to three levels: the local church, denominational staff, and theological study.

LOCAL LEVEL

Much criticism has been aimed toward Christian education in the local church. A great deal has been said about the Black church being a preaching church. Preaching is an indispensable element in Black Christian life and worship. But so is teaching. Black churches ought also to be teaching churches. Christian education is uniquely tied to living and carrying out the mission of the church.

The future of Christian education must affirm and emphasize the congregation's efforts: congregational self-determination, self-reliance, self-identity in the Black struggle for dignity.

All things considered, local churches have done a remarkable job to spiritually nurture the people of Allen. Congregation education has continued and new ministries have been developed. This continuing dedication needs to be recognized and celebrated.

DENOMINATIONAL LEVEL

Christian education will be impoverished. If the efforts of Christians are impoverished, a vital future for the church's educational ministry requires denominational support both human and financial.

Denominational educators should work together to develop new curriculum. The variety of educational images now shaping the field surely indicate that no one way will be sufficient.

Christian educators need to affirm the distinctive identity, perspectives and contributions of each cultural participant in the life of the connectional community. As a connectional community we need to fully value the gifts and graces of our culturally diverse constituency. The people of Allen live out their religious experience in a variety of cultural contexts: African American, African Caribbean, and Continental African.

However, the majority of Blacks in the A.M.E. Church share a common African-American cultural heritage. Most curriculum resources and materials produced by the denomination have reflected Euro-American or African-American cultural perspectives or practices.

Consequently, a predominantly African-American denomination like the A.M.E. Church produces curriculum resources to be used by an African-Caribbean and Continental African constituency who do not share the language, assumptions and practices of the majority cultural perspective in the denomination.

Black Christian educators need to explore the need of a multi-cultural curriculum which encourages church members to identify and affirm their own cultural heritage and to appreciate and respect that of others. It should facilitate the journey of faith particular cultural heritage resources.

ACADEMIC LEVEL

Current seminary education does not relate theological study to the life and mission of the congregation. Seminary curricula needs to shift its focus from the life and faith of the student to the life and faith of the local church. By making this shift, the seminary would be able to link theological inquiry to the spiritual growth of the congregation.

In addition, it is crucial that the academy and the church be in dialogue, and raise religious questions in a profound way. This unique responsibility will be a conduit for leading the church toward a radical learning to life. Otherwise it may as well move out of education. Seminaries must develop more practical structures and programs that have spiritual development as their objective.

The recovery of teaching can have a major impact on the ministry, mission and message of the church. Biblical illiteracy and theological ignorance can be overcome when both lay and clergy renew educational efforts in the life of the church in the world.

There are no easy answers to these challenges of the future. No matter how great the challenge, the church cannot afford to abandon Rev. Charles S. Smith's high standard: "Men study who without becoming wise and are learned without being useful."

PART II

Context of Christian Education Administration

CHAPTER 1

Understanding Christian Education in the A.M.E. Church

The education of African Methodist Christians is guided by the theological heritage of our denomination, grounded in scripture and lived and received through the experience of oppression. Christian education is a process that forms, informs, and transforms the people of Allen in Christ, and permeates the church's entire ministry. It takes place not simply at the local level, but in the annual conference, episcopal district and connectional level; whenever the church worships, prays, or plans. The educational ministry of the church must understand its task in broad terms.

AIMS OF CHRISTIAN EDUCATION

The fundamental goal of Christian education in the A.M.E. Church is the development of "Liberated achievers and fulfilled believers in Christ Jesus."[1]

To achieve this goal certain aims are required. They are largely derived from *The Book of Disciple* our doctrine, and the Episcopal Salutation on "The Nature and Mission of the Church."

These aims present a picture of what the development of liberated achievers and fulfilled believers in Christ entails. This list is suggestive of the major directions for the A.M.E. ministry of Christian education.

- Enlarge our grasp of the Bible.
- Appropriate and renew our tradition.
- Participate in the church's mission.

- Claim our ministry.
- Accept the struggle for human justice and dignity.
- Share the good news with all.
- Commune with God.
- Affirm the values of racial self-identity, self-development, self-reliance and self-help.

ENLARGE OUR GRASP OF THE BIBLE

What is the Bible? What is its place in the journey of faith? How is it to be used in Christian education? How does the Black Christian tradition inform the interpretation of scripture?

The Bible occupies a central place in the religious life of Blacks. It is from the Bible that many Black slaves learned to read, in order to find guidance, comfort, a word of hope, and the promise of their deliverance. It has been the source of inspiration for poetry, song, drama and worship. Black people have interpreted the Bible from their own experience, and have sought the Black church as a part of their identity formation.

Christian education's intention is to help persons enlarge their grasp of the Bible, to understand it more fully, to possess it more personally. This task calls for a critical reading, Black interpretation, and application of scripture to our life experiences. The task is informed by the tradition of the church and our personal and corporate Christian experience.

To reach this aim we must: give ourselves to Bible study; make use of the insights and tasks of biblical scholarship-interpretation; interpret scripture in the light of their place in the Bible as a whole and exploring them in relation to their original intentions and significance; rely on the Holy Spirit's guidance; and design a Bible literacy program.

APPROPRIATE AND RENEW OUR TRADITION

We receive our Christian identity through immersion in our tradition, one that includes our entire cultural heritage and connectional history. Who are we? Where have we come from? Where are we going? In confessions of faith, creeds, legacies, faiths, histories, symbols, stories, relationships, convictions and discipleship of the saints who have gone before us, we discover the sources to our own identity and tradition.

To be an A.M.E. Christian is to be an heir of our forefathers and mothers in the faith. Through the ages our ancestors have attempted to put their Christian experiences into word and song. Today we use their words and songs to guide and celebrate our own journey. In worship we share our motto, "God our Father, Christ our Redeemer, and Man our Brother." This historic statement helps us express our belief.

In our tradition there are several documents that help to inform our distinctive understanding of the Christian faith. We relied on the *Book of Worship*, the *Book of Discipline;* the Episcopal Salutation Historical Statement; the Doctrine and Discipline of the A.M.E. Church; and the Articles of Religion and Catechism.

To reach this aim we must:
- Help people appropriate the tradition through direct study.
- Develop curriculum resources for special connectional celebrations like Founders day.
- Facilitate the creative use of the hymns, stories and histories of the forbearers of the faith.

PARTICIPATE IN THE CHURCH'S MISSION

Faithful discipleship means taking part in the church's mission. As the congregation pursues its on-going quest for clarity about its purposes and ministries, education for mission occurs.

It also happens through member's Bible study of the mission of the church; and when members come together to plan ministries of service or action, to mobilize and train persons for this work.

Accepting the church's mission happens when members of the congregation become concerned for persons of other cultures or nations. When we take time to study and reflect on the social-political issues around the world, it enhances our growth and ultimately challenges and changes our perceptions and actions. Thus our aim in Christian Education is to involve church persons, of every age, in the congregation's mission life.

CLAIM OUR MINISTRY

For Christians our vocation is our calling from God, a calling that gives our entire life meaning and direction. This sense of vocation is nurtured in the community from childhood onward. In the adult years, it takes more specific form, as persons decide to take up particular ministries.

The Book of Discipline charges the Department of Christian Education through the Commission on Church Vocations with the responsibility for "developing a denominational strategy and plan for the recruiting, the training, and the placing of people in the pastoral ministry and other church vocations."

To achieve this aim our department must:
- help people explore the meaning of vocation,
- help people examine their own talents,
- help people listen for God's call and respond.

Since we are called to be a blessing to others, we must establish a wide range of ministries through which persons can carry out their vocation. We must promote greater appreciation for non-pastoral, specialized ministries, and assist clergy and lay to achieve professional excellence in such non-pastoral ministries, as educators, youth workers, and musicians through certification. The department intends to support and establish partnerships among the communions to further ecumenical dialogue and cooperative programming in Christian education and congregational ministries.

ACCEPT THE STRUGGLE FOR HUMAN JUSTICE and DIGNITY

Allen, Payne and other forbearers of the faith believed that Christ came in order to liberate us from injustice and oppression and to reconcile us to God. Christ Our Redeemer is part of the A.M.E. Church motto. Our tradition has lifted the liberation message of Jesus Christ primarily through preaching and worship.

Because the church has traditionally been a worshipping community, it has often failed to focus on the area of education in ministry. By viewing the curriculum of teaching and preaching as part of the practice of ministry, one can focus the church toward liberation.

Christian education is liberating when it helps members shape the reality within which they live, when members are empowered to engage in effective means of transforming processes, structures, policies and practices for justice both inside and outside the church.

In Black churches, Christian education has to be about keeping faith, doing justice, and building community. Therefore, social justice must become a primary agenda item. Christian education must encourage and enhance members' involvement in the struggle for justice and dignity.

TO SHARE THE GOOD NEWS WITH ALL

The tradition of evangelism bequeathed to African Methodism by William Paul Quinn still retains great relevance today. Diverse forms of sharing the good news are taking place. These forms include: spiritual discussion, general talk, visits, invitation to church, prayer for persons, building friendships, giving literature, and invitation to Bible study.

As Christians, we are under conviction to share the gospel with all. Christian education, along with other ministries of the church, is responsible for finding ways to share the good news with all. Moreover, Christian education must use church school and other forms of the teaching ministry, in reaching out to persons and helping people renew their faith journey.

TO COMMUNE WITH GOD

How do we commune with God? Communion happens in the corporate worship of the congregation. The Black church is traditionally a worshiping community. Blacks gather together in worship to praise God's loving and liberating presence in the midst of struggle. Like our African forebears, we worship with body, mind and soul. Communion with God through worship is a central need of African Methodist Christians.

The worship practice of African Methodist Christians has a variety of forms. One form is liturgical as a fixed pattern of practice. Another form is rooted in the proclamation of the word that serves as the basis of worship. The gifts of the spirit, especially speaking in tongues, has become another part of worship.

We begin to commune with God as we participate in a community who make such communion their habit. As the foremost shared experience in the local church, the weekly worship service is perhaps the chief setting for learning to commune with God.

There is perhaps no more powerful way to educate people in the faith than through this sharing of symbols, stories, music, creed and sacrament. Less formal worship experiences also help us deepen our communion with God: worship and prayer in church school classes, youth groups, adult groups and family programs.

Such settings provide opportunity to introduce the disciplines of communion with God, to explore the meaning of worship and prayer, to become familiar with the aids to worship, and to practice the needed skills.

The Christian Education department intends to pursue this aim by preparing materials that reinforce and reaffirm A.M.E. worship forms.

AFFIRM THE VALUES OF RACIAL SELF-RELIANCE, SELF-IDENTITY, SELF-HELP and SELF-DEVELOPMENT

The distinctive shape of our theological heritage can be seen in a constellation of emphases that display the liberating activity of God. It relies strongly on Richard Allen's writings and sermons to provide the framework of values which define our legacy.

Racial self-reliance, self-identity, self-help and self-development are interdependent. They allow for and positively encourage discipline. Jointly, they have provided a broad context for reflection.

These values "instruct" us as we carry forward our never-ending task of teaching in our church. Christian education has a role to play in teaching these values.

Through teaching we intend to guide persons of all ages in developing this framework of values. Our purpose is to help persons to improve and apply these values in many areas of practical concern—from personal life to church life, from peer relationships to world peace, from family life to criminal justice.

Many teaching events and curriculum materials will be designed around these concerns. In this process, we can discover what values are at stake in our lives. We will seek to teach in such a way that our common values will empower and enlighten the actions of all.

CHAPTER 2

Meaning of Curriculum in the A.M.E. Church

Christian education is a process that forms, informs, and transforms the people of Allen in Christ. The vocation of Christian education has been to instruct and liberate blacks, to instruct the people of Allen by creating a curriculum of tradition that flows from the life of the church, and to liberate the people of Allen by becoming co-workers with Christ in the ongoing work of freeing people from injustice.

What forms of curriculum have been used to instruct and liberate? In the A.M.E. Church our view of curriculum must be consistent with our basic biblical and theological foundations and educational aims. Our understandings of curriculum in Christian education must highlight our unity in the body of Christ. At the same time, our concept of curriculum must enable us to express our diversity opening and with integrity.

What meanings of curriculum have been traditioned to us through the years by the A.M.E. Church? Curriculum has multiple meanings.

Over the past two hundred years, African Methodist have developed their own meanings of curriculum. Such meanings of curriculum include: that which is taught; literacy; course of study; catechism; printed materials; and techniques, procedures and expertise.

Teaching is a way of invitation into the church's life, and handing on the tradition. The heritage of teaching within the A.M.E. Church begins with Richard Allen, founder and first bishop, who organized the first

African-American Sunday School at Mother Bethel, Philadelphia in 1794. His preaching and praying guided many people to grow in Christ. Richard Allen said he "saw a large field open in seeking and instructing my African brethren."[1]

Curriculum as literacy was given importance by Rev. Daniel A. Payne, called the Apostle of Education, who taught his own students from 1829 through 1835. Rev. Payne believed that literacy among African Americans meant self-improvement and moral reform. Payne was convinced that literacy not only gave the individual wider opportunities, but it would diminish prejudice against African Americans.

Curriculum as a course of study was also designed by Rev. Payne for ministers. In the late 19th century, Rev. Payne's dream of a four year course of study to be established in every annual conference, resulted in a standard series of books for ministers with a list of topics presented regularly in yearly cycles. Over a period of time, this became the accepted curriculum of A.M.E.s lasting into the present time.

Curriculum as catechism was developed by Rev. Henry McNeil Turner. In the late 18th century, Rev. Turner saw the need for basic instruction in the tradition. The meaning of catechism as instruction was seen by Turner as a fundamental task of teaching.

Turner's Catechism was doctrinal, centered on the Articles of Faith; and it was historical, centered on the life and mission of the church. Memorization of the answers to such questions as "What is meant by the Brotherhood of Man?" "What is prayer?" "What is the African Methodist Episcopal Church?" "What is God?" was a staple of African Methodist diet for several generations.

Curriculum as printed materials was affirmed by Rev. Charles S. Smith, M.D. His most notable contribution to African Methodism was the establishment of the Sunday School Union and Publishing House in 1884.

The work of the Union consisted of primarily publishing the periodicals for the church school as well as literary works, editorials, speeches and addresses. Smith was not satisfied with the pace of growth. He often said, "Our literature is yet to be produced."[2]

In the 20th century church school, curriculum forms became influenced by public education. The forms include such activities as workshops, seminars, and individualized learning; such are the A.M.E. curriculum practices.

All of these curriculum practices reflect an understanding that the curriculum or what was taught, originated from a printed base. Curriculum now began to exist as a text, or as a set of texts, designed to help people know the tradition and obey the laws.

When we take these factors into account, multiple meanings, and draw on the strengths in the positions cited, what conclusion can we draw at this time about the nature of curriculum from this historical overview?

Until very recently, the main thrust in curriculum thinking and planning has been the belief that curriculum was the printed material and nothing more. In addition, the church school was seen as the only aspect of church life as educative.

Another main thrust has been to lift the tradition of the church through instruction and to lift the liberation message of Jesus Christ through preaching and worship. This in turn lead to the absence of the theme of liberation from curriculum resources and materials. The teaching curriculum needs to focus on liberation, a theology of education that liberates guiding people to engage in social change.

A shift in curriculum thinking and planning has become evident in recent years. Black Christian educators and others involved in the Christian education ministry, are developing curriculum resources and materials that reflect and perpetuate Black cultural values and perspectives.

This is a curriculum of teaching, understanding, worshiping, praying, and serving, from the Black Christian tradition, it is a curriculum that teaches the Allenite values of self-dignity, self-reliance, self-identity and self-development; that teaches about the African presence in the Bible; that is prophetic; that reflects the cultural and historical experience of Blacks connectionally; and that sees all aspects of church life as educative and educating, and thus part of curriculum.

In summary, the early efforts of Christian education of many African Methodist Christians grew out of the concern to improve Blacks condition of Biblical illiteracy and theological ignorance. The curriculum forms involved a focus on teaching activities and did not see other aspects of church life as educative. We must facilitate the education of Blacks in ways that they experience God's liberating power, Jesus' empowering love and the Holy Spirit's everlasting strength.

CHAPTER 3

Learning, Organizing and Planning Christian Education in the A.M.E. Church

THE SETTING OF TEACHING AND LEARNING

Christian education permeates the church's entire ministry. It takes place in three centers of teaching and learning: teaching and education on behalf of the whole denomination; scholarly and theological inquiry and clergy education; and practical theological reflection and lay education.[1]

BISHOPS AND DENOMINATIONAL AGENCIES

In the A.M.E. Church, the first of these centers is found in the connectional bodies and episcopal leaders who represent the church as a whole. Bishops and denominational agencies carry out the teaching ministry. They gather up the wisdom that is dispersed throughout the church and pass it on to our members and congregations.

Their task focuses on the activity of setting forth those teachings by which our church identifies itself as a community. This involves the transmission and preservation of the central elements of the heritage of our community. Thus, teaching A.M.E. beliefs and practices provides continuity with the original mission, ministry and message of Richard Allen.

UNIVERSITIES AND SEMINARIES

The second center is largely focused on our seminaries and universities and the professional theologians on our faculties. They represent the intellectual center of our church and bring intellectual reflection and criticism to bear on worship, preaching, teaching and care of the souls.

Their task necessitates reinterpreting and relating our tradition to contemporary connectional life. Our theologians have attempted to convince their students and the denomination that the church must reclaim the liberating aspects of its heritage to be relevant today. Their thinking and writing enhances and challenges congregational and denominational life. Sometimes tension between bishops, leaders of agencies and theologians emerge over what role they play in the church's teaching ministry. What these roles are and how they are to be related is a matter yet to be determined.

LOCAL CONGREGATIONS

Theological reflection gives members of congregations the opportunity to appropriate the tradition. The faith in comes alive as it is linked to the histories and stories of our congregations. Every congregation knits together the unique events and experiences of its pasts and present and projects a sense of the future that its living toward.

One of the most important tasks facing our pastors in helping our congregations become centers of teaching and learning is to understand its life. The setting for Christian education in the local A.M.E. Church is both formal and informal. In a formal setting the structures, expectations and procedures are apparent. Planning is very deliberate. For the most part, the formal settings for Christian education are those educational programs designed for systematic study and reflection.

Indeed, it is through the Sunday morning settings of the church school that most congregations carry out the largest part of their educational ministry. The Sunday school is a formal, ongoing, basic setting for systematic study and reflection by all ages.

Our formal settings also include Bible study groups, vacation church schools, workshops, seminars, and meetings. But many of our other settings are informal. Increasingly our churches are finding great value in less structured, more personal, more relational gatherings for education.

A variety of forms include fellowship meetings, celebrations, retreats, camping, family experiences, outings, trips, and seasonal festivals. Thus, Christian education includes the totality of these educational settings, formal and informal.

ORGANIZATION OF CHRISTIAN EDUCATION

The Department of Christian Education develops the general A.M.E. plan for teaching and learning. This is one of the ways the department fulfills the responsibility assigned to it by *The Discipline*.

Christian education administration takes place at five levels in the church:

- The connectional level fashions, interprets and recommends the general A.M.E. plan for Christian education.
- The Episcopal District level. Here Christian education administration is guided by the bishop and implemented by the district director of Christian education.
- The presiding elder's level implements the presiding elder's own initiatives or those of the bishop.
- The annual conference level. Here the Commission on Christian Education plans and programs. Program initiatives are derived from the connectional, episcopal or conference level.
- The local church level. Here Christian administration is guided by the pastor, administered by local director, and implemented by the church school and other agencies and organizations.

GENERAL CONFERENCE

GENERAL BOARD

COMMISSION ON
CHRISTIAN EDUCATION

CHRISTIAN EDUCATION
CONNECTIONAL OFFICE

EPISCOPAL DISTRICT CHRISTIAN DIRECTOR
(appointed by Bishop)

ANNUAL CONFERENCE

PRESIDING ELDER'S DISTRICT

LOCAL CHRISTIAN EDUCATION DIRECTOR
(appointed by Pastor)

PLANNING CHRISTIAN EDUCATION

The church school is an essential component in the ministry of the congregation. The *Book of Discipline* states that in each local church there shall be a church school "so organized as to discharge its responsibility for the religious development of its entire constituency, in accordance with the policies of the Department of Christian Education, and the editorial division and with the concurrence of the pastor." (163:7N).[2]

It is the Department of Christian Education in cooperation with the Department of Publication that develops the general A.M.E. plan for the church school, which comes into being through three interrelated stages of planning.

The plan is designed, interpreted and recommended to church leaders through teaching, training and resources developed by the Christian education department.

A second stage of planning for the church school occurs in each church by the local Christian education director, church school superintendent and pastor. Here, based on review of local needs, the general plan is reworked and refined. A local plan for Christian education is designed as an integral part of the congregation's whole mission.

A third stage of planning takes place in each department, club, auxiliary and organization in the church. Members and leaders join in shared responsibility for the life of the church. In response to the needs of each group, particular plans for education are laid. Thus, in each session of every group education takes place.

At each stage of planning for the church school we hope to reach the aims of Christian education. That involves asking four important questions:

WHO will be involved in the planning, teaching and learning experiences? How many are to be included, of what age or gender?

WHAT is to be taught and learned in order to achieve the purposes of Christian education? What is the curriculum?

WHEN is the best time for gathering people in an educational venture? How many sessions? How long? How often? What hours?

WHERE will planning take place?

Conducting the planning at a different location, away from the church, may stimulate fresh ways of seeing the relationship of the gospel and life. Retreat settings certainly provide an environment that enhances educational aims.

PART III

Content of Christian Education: Foundations for Christian Education

CHAPTER 4

Christian Education in the A.M.E. Church: Some Foundational Principles

Christian education in the African Methodist Episcopal Church has traditionally been governed by three foundational principles reflected in it's literature and tradition. These principles are that Christian education must be: Spiritually Nurturing, Culturally Relevant, and Denominationally Specific.

SPIRITUALLY NURTURING

This principle of Christian education reminds us that we are a part of the Universal Church of which Jesus Christ is Lord. In this general sense, Christian education is intended to lift up, in an instructive and spiritually nurturing manner, the elemental and basic beliefs of the Christian faith. The purpose of which is to strengthen the individual in his/her faith. In a general sense, Christian education exists to help in the formation of the moral life of people intentionally and intimately involved in the life of the Christian Community. In this community, God is considered to be the Creator and Jesus Christ the Center.

In the A.M.E. Church, as in any other Christian community, children and adults learn and assimilate the values, convictions, interpretation, and action of the faith community. This is accomplished through worship and learning the *stories, symbols, rituals,* and beliefs of the Universal Church of Jesus Christ.

One such symbol and ritual that is important to all Christians is baptism. This practice is related to God's activity of liberation in the Old Testament where God led the people of Israel through the Red Sea, "figuring thereby holy baptism." Participation in this ritual, as a child or as an adult, calls forth the role of Christian education as the means by which one is led to understand the significance of baptism for membership in Christ's church.

In the case of children, Christian education aids in spiritual nurture through Sunday school, parental instruction, or special classes for confirmation. Such classes could lead children to affirm the faith into which they were baptized. Christian education serves spiritual nurture by leading the adult to understand the true significance of "being regenerated and born anew of water and of the Holy Ghost."

Another important ritual of the faith which Christian education can help interpret and thereby help individual nurture is the Lord's Supper. It, especially in the General Confession, relates a number of ideas that are important for the spiritual health of the individual; i.e., repent are in love and charity with your neighbor, intend to lead a new life. Of crucial significance are the two major symbols: the Bread, and the Wine. For African Methodism, as with other denominations, the bread and wine become symbols of the broken body and shed blood of Christ. This act is participated in with an act of thankfulness and in remembrance.

Crucial to understanding Christian education's role in spiritual nurture is to realize that nurture comes from within a loving and instructing community. For a church, community points to the ecclesia which is used in the New Testament to designate those who have: accepted the preaching of the gospel of Christ; participated in the sacraments of baptism and the Lord's Supper; and received the gift of the Holy Spirit and gather for common worship and celebration. Christian education then exists in large measure to aid the church in its role as spiritual nurturer. Christian education in the A.M.E. Church must also be culturally relevant, related to people of African heritage in this country and abroad.

CULTURALLY RELEVANT

Education does not occur in a vacuum. What and how one learns is dependent upon the cultural perspective one brings to the learning process. This means that the stories, rituals, symbols and values, which are so much a part of the Christian church, must be related and filtered through the eyes, hearts and minds of people who have been oppressed and disinherited by the majority culture.

To be culturally relevant, Christian education must be translated into the spirit and world view of the African American experience. This principle is evident in the history surrounding the establishment of our own Zion. Richard Allen was generally convinced that Christianity was the religion most relevant to the Christian education in the A.M.E. Church must also be culturally relevant to the African people in this country. More specifically he felt that African people needed structure and discipline and that Methodism was the most helpful cultural expression of Christianity. Moreover, he felt that American Methodism should be given an "African hue" by bringing to bear the experience of oppression and the desire for the reality of the liberating presence of Christ in the daily lives of African people. This "African hue" is reflected in the distinctive style in preaching, singing and worshiping theology found in A.M.E. churches everywhere.

To speak of Christian education's responsibility to be culturally relevant is to acknowledge that the A.M.E. Church is an international church and as such diversity is a key theme to be explored and explained. Diversity and unity are the common poles in the African Methodist experience.

Worship is tied together by the common witness to Christ and Christ's ultimate significance to the individual. This common witness in worship would be expressed differently in the Caribbean in Africa, in Guyana, in Great Britain and other places of African Methodism. Thus even within the USA, there are diversities of worship experience because of regional differences. The diversity should be interpreted as a peculiar strength of African Methodistm. Our Zion has the responsibility of interpreting this diversity in a manner that promotes unity, not uniformity.

DENOMINATIONALLY SPECIFIC

Christian education must be related to the universal principles of the Christian faith, but also must be related to a specific denominational expression. Christian education in the A.M.E. Church must deal with the education of the people called African Methodist Episcopal. This education must take the lead in helping the denomination identify, express, develop, and organize what the cardinal values and virtues of African Methodism are in terms of belief, history, theology and polity that should be passed on to each generation.

One such value is that of self-help and elevation of the race. In explaining the reason for establishing Wilberforce University, Daniel Alexander Payne stated in 1857: "This benevolent scheme is based on the supposition that the colored man must, for the most part, be the educator and elevator of his own race in this and other lands."

For Payne, this virtue is related to the primary one which is to provide a moral and theological foundation for the pursuit of the life to which God calls the individual.

Christian education, in its task of being denominationally specific, can take the lead in helping identify and develop the cardinal values that are the core essence of African Methodism. This assumes an important research and interpretive function. Christian education in cooperation with A.M.E. scholars and pastors can serve an important role in defining the denominational heritage and contribution of African Methodism and relating it to contemporary issues.

Two issues are apparent: First, spiritual foundation in the midst of a secular society deals with the formation, nurturing and maintenance of the individual's inner life—the life of the soul. This concern may be stated in the form of questions. What does it mean to be a worshipping, praying and thinking African Methodist in a society increasingly secular? How do we form, express and interpret the core essence of African Methodism to the young A.M.E. in our international church?

The second issue is the social engagement of the question of ethics. As a believer and a member of Christ's church, what am I to do when confronted by socio-ethical problems such as racism, sexism, abortion, euthanasia and institutionalism?

As a beliver, and as a member of Christ's church as reflected in African Methodism, what ought I do in the face of the capitulation to the values of rampant consumerism, which creates and sustains distance from the distressed African, African American masses in the USA, the Caribbean and Africa?

In conclusion, Christian education occurs in this tension-filled process of relating the universal claims of the Christian faith to the specific cultural and denominational claims of the African, African American and African Methodist people respectively. In this manner, African Methodism can come to grips with itself and its soul and will work towards true redemption and liberation.

CHAPTER 5

"God Our Father, Christ Our Redeemer, Man Our Brother" – A Theological Interpretation

What is connected with the conditions of our lives? Many scholars today believe that all knowledge is determined by social conditions and is, therefore, subject to error. The implication is that no one can claim that his or her thinking is completely objective. What people regard as true and real depends partly or wholly upon how they perceive their social and political interests.

This is true even of our thinking about God. What people think about God and Jesus Christ cannot be separated from their social, economic, and political existence. This statement may be shocking to theologians and other church people who would like to believe that *religious* ideas are somewhat purer than other ideas and less influenced by world circumstances. But if they read the Bible carefully, they discover that divine revelation, so far from exempting theology from world circumstance, requires our involvement in the world in order to perceive God's truth.

The God of the Bible is not a philosophical principle, nor an absolute idea as defined in Greek philosophy. The biblical God is the God of history whose truth is known in the liberation of slaves from bondage. Truth therefore is not an idea, but a divine event which invades human history and bestows freedom in wretched places.

Knowledge about this truth depends upon our socio-political situation; that is, whether we are on the side of God's liberating presence or on the side of the status quo. If the latter, then there is no way for us to understand the meaning of biblical faith.

Faith is inseparably connected with obedience to the God of history. Unless we are prepared to live according to the claims of faith, then we cannot understand the meaning of its truth. Because Pharaoh was not in the socio-political situation for the hearing of divine truth, he did not understand the meaning of God's proclamation to "Let my people go."

The same was equally true of the people of Israel when God spoke through the prophets, insisting that the poor were not created for injustice and humiliation. In the New Testament, Jesus made a similar point: "Those who are well have no need of a physician, but those who are sick; I came not to call the righteous, but sinners."

Because the Kingdom of God involves a total commitment to the liberating presence of Jesus, people who occupy a certain socio-political security in this present world cannot make the needed leap of faith into God's coming future. Only the poor, those with nothing to lose and everything to gain, can hear the truth and thus live according to it's claim upon humanity.

If what we say about the connection between thought and social existence is correct, then the theology of the A.M.E. Church as defined by its motto, "God Our Father, Christ Our Redeemer, Man Our Brother," must be analyzed within the social and political context of the church's origin.

This motto cannot and ought not to mean the same thing as the white Methodist Church when it speaks of God, Jesus Christ, and brotherhood. To be sure, the A.M.E. Church accepted the policy and doctrines of Methodism as defined by John Wesley and the articles of religion. But there is no evidence that the A.M.E.s doctrines of God, Jesus Christ, and humanity are the same as those of the white Methodists.

The reason why most people think that there is no doctrinal difference between the A.M.E. Church and white Methodism is that they have defined christian doctrines according to the conceptualization of white theological textbooks. Since there are no existing theological textbooks on A.M.E. doctrine, people may conclude that the A.M.E.s are a church without a theology. (Unfortunately many A.M.E.s themselves have internalized and accepted that assumption.)

But I contend that the meaning of a people's faith is not conclusively decided by what they write in textbooks or even the conceptual content of their sermons. Faith is defined by obedience. That is, I know what your words mean by what you do.

Meaning is defined by action. Since Richard Allen and Daniel Payne did not act the same way as their white contemporaries, I must conclude that they invested in the words, "God," "Christ," and "brotherhood," with different meaning from those of the white preachers of the Methodist Church. It is with this assumption in mind that we search out the original meaning of the A.M.E. Church's motto: "God Our Father, Christ Our Redeemer, Man Our Brother."

GOD OUR FATHER. To know what the founders of the A.M.E. Church meant by this phrase, it is necessary to penetrate the social and political circumstances that brought their existence into being. For Richard Allen, God was not a philosophic idea but a spiritual presence in his life that affirmed the dignity of his personhood in the midst of slavery. He speaks of his encounter with God with apocalyptic imagination: "I cried..., and all of a sudden my dungeon shook, my chains flew off... (for) the Lord had heard my prayers and pardoned all my sins."[1]

This experience made it impossible for Allen to remain a slave and to accept second-class membership in St. George Methodist Church. The fullest implication of his conversion experience may not have been known to Allen at the time; and he, perhaps, did not have the theological sophistication to articulate the depths of its meaning. But if thought is connected with action, then we can observe his actions as a clue to the meaning of Allen's conversion.

He bought his freedom, entered the ministry, and later founded the first independent black Methodist Church as a protest against segregated worship. Bishop Frederick Talbot's description of Allen as "God's Fearless Prophet"[2] is accurate and appropriate, because Allen took the risk to make a distinctive theological assessment of God's presence in the world. For Allen, God was the Father of all peoples of this earth. Why then did white "christians" treat Blacks as second-class people of God? The God of the Bible is no respecter of persons.

Richard Allen's understanding of God as the God of blacks as well as whites was the key to his refusal to accept white people's domination of black people. If God is the God of all, how then can segregation and slavery be justified? The God of the Bible is the ground of freedom and the source of Black people's affirmation of their personhood.

Reflecting on the St. George experience, Allen said it well: "We all went out of the church in a body, and they were no more plagued with us in the church."[3] Bishop Daniel Payne, from whom the motto, "God Our Father, Christ Our Redeemer, Man Our Brother," is derived, recognized the contradiction between the christian God and American slavery.

Not only could he not understand how professed christians could own slaves, but he also questioned the justice and righteousness of God. In western theology and philosophy, this contradiction is called the problem of theodicy and many hours have been expended trying "rationally" to reconcile God's absolute goodness and power with the presence of evil in the world.

But for Bishop Payne and the black constituency he represented, black suffering and the absurdities of faith arising out of it were not mainly problems of reason in an abstract sense of the term. The contradiction of black suffering with faith in the God of the Bible did not have its origin in the reading of the philosophies of Augustine and David Hume. The contradiction of black suffering with the christian faith happened in black people's experience of God at prayer meeting on Sunday night and of the slave driver in the field on Monday morning.

Payne wondered how these two realities could be reconciled.

> *Sometimes it seemed as though some wild beast had plunged his fangs into my heart, and was squeezing out it's life-blood. Then I began to question the existence of God, and to say: "If He does exist, is He just? If so, why does He suffer one race to oppress and enslave another, to rob them by unrighteous enactments of rights, which they hold most dear and sacred"? Sometimes I wished for the lawmakers that Nero wished, "that the Romans had but one neck." I would be the man to sever the head from its shoulders. Again said I: "Is there no God"?*[4]

These are the words of a man who could not accept slavery as consistent with God as the creator of all peoples. Slavery must mean that God does not exist. But Payne could not accept atheism. It was too easy, a rational cop-out. It merely justifies the right of the powerful to rule over the weak. Only people who are in power or who have resigned themselves to accept oppression can accept a rational solution to the problem of evil.

Furthermore, Payne was a man of struggle who had already

encountered God in the fight for freedom. The experience of God cannot be invalidated merely because God's behavior does not measure up to our rational conceptions of justice. Such an idea removes the sense of mystery and awe from divine presence and places our rationality above God.

It was this sense of divine mystery which Bishop Payne affirmed in the context of black suffering, knowing that God, the Father of all, will effect His justice in His own future.

> *But then (writes Payne) there came into my mind those solemn words: "With God one day is as a thousand years and a thousand years as one day. Trust in Him, and He will bring slavery and its outrages to an end." These words from the spirit world acted on my troubled soul like water on a burning fire, and my aching heart was soothed and relieved from its burden of woes.*[5]

With Allen and Payne as its early leaders, the A.M.E. Church affirmed black dignity by insisting that the God of the Bible was the Creator and Father of all peoples. This assumption was the starting point of its theology, giving black people the courage to live as children of the Almighty by refusing to accept second-class status in the white Methodist Church.

Unfortunately, the contemporary A.M.E. Church has not always remained true to the faith of its mothers and fathers. Let's fact it: We as a church have forgotten about the fatherhood and the motherly role that God has played in the lives of black people. Like Israel who forgot about the God of the Exodus, and began to run after the Baal gods of Canaan; we, too, have pursued the God of religion and the faith of the rich.

Unlike Allen, we know that God has a special concern for the poor and the black, we are often embarrassed by our blackness and no longer appreciate the *African* origin of our faith. Unlike Bishop Henry M. Turner, who in 1898 asserted that "God is a Negro," we are ashamed to define God as black. How can black people know that God is their father, if He is not black? How can the poor know that poverty is an injustice against God, if God is not a father for the fatherless and a mother for the motherless.

The problem with the contemporary A.M.E. Church is that its ministers are more concerned about who is going to be elected a bishop in 1976 than about the poor blacks who are being oppressed and humiliated in racist America. I do not intend to tell the bishops and the ministers how to run the church. But to become an A.M.E. bishop or to accept the call into God's ministry is to accept a special responsibility defined by the scripture and the tradition of Allen and Payne.

If we take the scripture seriously as defined by these Black fathers, what else can we say except the A.M.E. Church "ain't what it used to be." It used to be a church whose primary mission was to liberate black people from the conditions of oppression. It used to be a church in which the office of the bishop was one of service.

Daniel Payne, turned down the invitation to become a bishop in 1848 because he did not feel himself worthy. He was elected in 1852 not because he sought the office, but because his brethren insisted that he was the person for the job. Can you imagine some A.M.E. minister turning down the bishopric today because he felt unfit?

Unfortunately, it seems that the beginning and the end of the A.M.E. Church's significance is in the office of the bishop. This office has often taken the place of God and usurped His fatherhood over the people. Therefore, what the A.M.E. Church needs is to re-think its mission in the light of the fatherly role of God, so that it can better serve as the liberating agent of God in the world.

CHRIST OUR REDEEMER. Allen, Payne, and the other founders of the A.M.E. Church had something specifically in mind when they affirmed that Christ was their redeemer. They understood this affirmation as connected with the fatherhood of God. God, the Father of all humankind, sent His only begotten Son into the world in order that we might be saved. That is, Christ came in order to liberate us from sin and to reconcile us to God. Conversion was the actualization of this experience of salvation.

The founders of the A.M.E. Church held no church councils on christology and soteriology. Unlike the bishops at Nicea, Constantinople, and Chalcedon, the A.M.E. bishops did not ask about the ontological status of the Son's relation to the Father, or whether the Holy Spirit proceeded from the Father alone or the Father and the Son. Neither did they ask about the status of the humanity and divinity in Jesus' person.

The A.M.E. Church has not produced theologians who reflected on the doctrine of the atonement as found in Anselm, Abelard, and more recently in Gustaf Aulen of Sweden. Such problems as defined by the early church councils or by contemporary theologians on christology and soteriology were not and are not today the problems of black people.

Although I respect what happened at Nicea and Chalcedon and the theological input of the early church fathers on christology, that source alone is inadequate for finding out the meaning of black folks' Jesus. It is alright to say as did Athanasius that the Son is *homoousios* (one substance with the Father), especially if one has a taste for Greek philosophy and a feel for the importance of intellectual distinctions. But the homoousios question is not a black question. Blacks do not ask whether Jesus is one with the Father or divine and human, although the orthodox formulations are implied in their language. They ask whether Jesus is walking with them, whether they can call upon the telephone of prayer and tell him all about their troubles.

It is not that blacks did not regard the homoousios question as important. They simply did not know that Jesus' status was in question. If the christological question were put to them, I am sure that the average A.M.E. Church member would respond something like this: "Go on, boy, and leave me alone. I know who Jesus is, and you're not going to confuse me with your education. I know who Jesus is because I just talked with Him, and you come asking me all them silly questions about... what's that big word you used? ...Homo what? Don't you let your books get you confused, boy"!

This comment, constructed from a conversation I had with a black church member, should not be taken as a put-down of education or as a belittling of disciplined theological thinking. (It is not unchristian or anti-black to attend college and seminary.) The comment was merely an affirmation that one does not meet Jesus through reading books. One meets Him in the concreteness of life, in the midst of suffering and through the struggle of liberation. Allen and Payne met Jesus in the contradictions of life, where the "load was heavy" and the way was narrow.

To be sure, Athanasius' assertion about the status of the Son in the Godhead is important for the church's continued christological investigations. But we must not forget that Athanasius' question about the Son's status in relation to the Father did not arise in the historical context of slave codes and overseers. If he had been a black slave in America, I am sure he would have asked a different set of questions. He might have asked about the status of the Son in relation to slave holders.

Perhaps the same is true of Martin Luther's concern about the ubiquitous presence of Jesus Christ at the Lord's Table. Without diminishing the importance of Luther's theological concern I contend that if he had been born a black slave and had experienced the brutalizing presence of white society in the "land of the free and the home of the brave," I am sure that his first concern would not have been the manner of Jesus' presence at the Lord's Table, but the manner of His presence in the slave's cabin. Could the slaves expect Jesus to be with them as they tried to survive the whip and pistol?

My point is that one's social and historical context decide not only the questions we address to God and Jesus but also the mode or form of the answers given to the questions. Therefore, to understand what the A.M.E. Church meant by the phrase "Christ Our Redeemer," we need not search the records of the ancient councils. Rather, we must look in the historical context of black slavery and see how black people read the Bible in the light of their slavery.

Allen and Payne did not have the luxury of debating about Jesus, but they struggled with Jesus, trying to figure out whether the Lord would redeem black people from the pains of slavery. Therefore, for these early black ministers, Jesus was not the object or product of philosophical speculation. He was a spiritual and historical presence in black life, bestowing upon black people the strength to "keep on keepin' on," because they had "to make the best of a bad situation."

Jesus was the divine power in their situation who could smooth out the rough places in their lives. They sometimes called Him "wheel in the middle of a wheel," "the Rose of Sharon," the "lily of the valley," and "the bright and mornin' star." In the words of an old spiritual: "He's King of Kings, and Lord of Lords, Jesus Christ, the first and the last. No man works like Him."

This is the christological matrix in which the A.M.E. Church's view of Jesus as the Redeemer ought to be understood. Christ as our Redeemer means that He is black people's liberator. With Jesus as the captain of the "Old Ship of Zion," we are free to struggle against injustice and oppression. Let us hope that the contemporary A.M.E. Church will return to it's tradition by taking seriously Jesus' claim that He came "to preach good news to the poor," "to proclaim release to the captives and recovering of sight to the blind," and "to set at liberty those who are oppressed."

MAN OUR BROTHER. Brotherhood and sisterhood are grounded in the fatherhood and the motherly presence of God in black life. If God is the Father of all and is present as a mother for the motherless, then all people are in fact created equal; that is, as brothers and sisters before God and humanity. If Jesus Christ is the redeemer and liberator of all, then the distinctions between blacks and whites make no sense from a theological or a political standpoint.

The brotherhood and sisterhood of humanity as grounded in the creative and redeeming presence of the divine Spirit was the source of Daniel Payne's affirmations:

> "I am opposed to slavery, not because it enslaves the black man, but because it enslaves man. And were all the slaveholders in this land men of color, and the slaves white men, I would be as thorough and uncompromising an abolitionist as I now am; for whatever and whenever I may see a being in the form of a man, enslaved by his fellowman, without respect to his complexion, I shall lift up my voice to plead his cause, against all claims of his proud oppressor; and I shall do it not merely from the sympathy which man feels towards suffering man, but because God, the living God, who I dare not disobey, has commanded me to open my mouth for the dumb, and plead the cause of the oppressed."[6]

Payne's protest against slavery was not grounded in any belief in the essential goodness of humanity as defined by the 18th century Enlightenment and articulated by many white abolitionists in the 19th century America. Payne's condemnation was derived from the biblical view that God created all peoples as brothers and sisters. Therefore, no race of people has the right to enslave another. Reflecting on Psalm 8, he writes:

> "This being God created but little lower than the angels, and crowned him with glory and honor; but slavery hurls him down from his elevated position, to the level of brutes! Strikes this crown of glory from his head, and fastens upon his neck the galling yoke! And compels him to labor like an ox, through summer's sun and winter's snow, with renunciation."[7]

The theme that all people are brothers and sisters was a dominant theme in the A.M.E. Church through the 19th century, during and after legal slavery. Payne, felt so strongly about the equality of people that he suspended one of his ministers for refusing to accept a white woman into membership of an A.M.E. Church.

With a different emphasis, the brotherhood and sisterhood of people before God was the ground of Bishop Henry M. Turner's protest against the Georgia House of Representatives for expelling black members of that body:

> "I wish the members of this House to understand the position I take. I hold that I am a member of this body. Therefore. ... I shall neither fawn nor cringe before any party, nor stoop to beg them for my rights. Some of my colored fellow members, in the course of their remarks, took occasion to appeal to the sympathies of members on the opposite side, and to eulogize their character for magnanimity. It reminds me very much ... of slaves begging under the lash. I am here to demand my rights, and to hurl thunderbolts at the men who would dare cross the threshold of my manhood."[8]

Then Turner moves to a deeper theological level and sees the connection between his humanity and God's fatherhood:

> "You may expel us, gentlemen, by your votes, today; but, while you do it, remember that there is a just God in Heaven, whose All-Seeing Eye beholds alike the acts of the oppressor and the oppressed, and who, despite the machinations of the wicked, never fails to vindicate the cause of Justice and the sanctity of His own handiwork."[9]

Would that we had more A.M.E. ministers and bishops who understood the gospel with the insights of Henry M. Turner. Why is it that we have so many ministers who do not understand the significance of Black Theology, Black Christ and Black God when the A.M.E. Church is African in origin, and its early leaders were unqualifiedly identified with the liberation of black people? Why is it that the blackness of our faith is not expressed in our creeds, polity, sermons and songs?

It appears that we really believe the white contention that A.M.E. Church is nothing but a white church with black members. As long as we express our faith like white people, repeating their creeds and singing their songs, and entering into consultation with them about church union with little or no reference to color in the definition of our faith, then black radicals are correct in their contention that christianity is the white man's religion and it must be destroyed along with the white oppressor.

I have contended otherwise by pointing to Allen, Payne and Turner. But, unfortunately, there is little evidence coming from the contemporary A.M.E. Church which contradicts the opinion of the radicals' observation. I contend that the contemporary A.M.E. Church must make a decision about its mission. Either it should define its mission with the poor and the black by emphasizing God's will to liberate the oppressed from bondage or else it should define its mission in terms of the cultural and political values of white America. By refusing to accept the first alternative, the church automatically opts for the second.

I think the first alternative is the only choice for people who take seriously the scripture and the A.M.E. Church tradition. To create a church that is identified with the value-system of America is to deny everything that scripture represents. To people who claim that they do not see the God of the Bible as the One who is for the liberation of the oppressed and against the proud and the mighty, then I can only say that we must be reading different Bibles.

I would make the same claim for the A.M.E. Church during the time of Allen, Payne and Turner. Were they to re-appear on the scene, they would not recognize the Church they helped to create. They founded a church for the liberation of poor black people. Thus the choice of name, the *African Methodist Episcopal Church*, was no accident.

The name reflected the members of a church who believed that God is the Father of all, that Christ is the Redeemer of all, and that all people are brothers and sisters in the faith. If this theme represents the spirit and ethos of the present-day A.M.E. Church, then we are doing a good job of keeping it a secret. Because I believe in the A.M.E. Church, I challenge us all to renew our spirit by going back to the "old time religion" of Allen and Payne, both of whom represent the liberating force of God's presence among black people.

NOTES

CHAPTER 1
1. George L. Champion, Sr., *The Christian Education for the African American Church* (West Palm Beach, Fl: Broadway, 1990).

CHAPTER 2
1. Richard Allen, *The Life Experience and Gospel Labors* (Nashville: Abingdon, 1960).
2. Rev. C. S. Smith, M.D., *The Literature of the A.M.E. Church* (Bloomington, IL, 1982), p. 7.

CHAPTER 3
1. Richard Robert Osmer, *A Teachable Spirit* (Westminister/John Knox Press, Louisville, Kentucky, 1990), p. 179.
2. *The A.M.E. Book of Discipline* (AMEC Publishing House, Nashville, TN, 1988).

CHAPTER 5
1. Richard Allen, *The Life Experience and Gospel Labors* (Nashville: Abingdon, 1960), p. 15, 16.
2. See Frederick Talbot, *God's Fearless Prophet: The Story of Richard Allen*, a pamphlet.
3. Allen, op. cit., p. 25.
4. Daniel A. Payne, *Recollections of Seventy Years* (New York: Arno Press, reprint, 1969), p. 28.
5. Ibid.
6. "Bishop Daniel Alexander Payne's Protestation of American Slavery," *Journal of Negro History*, Vol. LII (1967), p. 60.
7. Ibid.
8. Cited in Herbert Aptheker (ed.), *A Documentary History of The Negro People in the United States*, Vol. II (New York: Citadel Press, 1968), p. 69.
9. Ibid., p. 571.

BIBLIOGRAPHY

GENERAL BLACK CHURCH HISTORY AND THEOLOGY

Cone, Cecil. *The Identity Crisis in Black Theology.* Nashville: A.M.E. Sunday School Union, 1975.

Cone, James. *For My People.* New York: Maryknoll, Orbis Books, 1982.

Lincoln, C. Eric. *Race Religion and the Continuing American Dilemma.* New York: Hill and Wang, 1984.

Wilmore, Gayraud, S. *Black Religion and Black Randicalism.* New York: Maryknoll, Orbis Books, 1973, 1983.

Woodson, Carter G. *The History of the Negro Church.* Washington, D.C.: Associated Publishers, 1921, 1945, 1972.

A.M.E. CHURCH HISTORY

Berry, Lewellyn L. *A Century of Missions of the A.M.E. Church, 1840-1940.* New York: Guttenburg Printing Company, 1942.

Gaines, Wesley J. *African Methodism in the South.* Chicago: Afro-American Press, Reprint 1969.

George, Carol V.R. *Segregated Sabbaths.* New York: Oxford University Press, 1973.

Gregg, Howard D. *History of the A.M.E. Church.* Nashville: A.M.E. Sunday School Union, 1980.

Hill, Kenneth H. *Charles Spencer Smith - A Portrait: Sable Son of God.* A.M.E.C. Publishing, 1993.

Jenifer, John T. *Centennial Retrospect History of the African Methodist Episcopal Church.* Nashville: A.M.E. Sunday School Union, 1918.

Johnson, Walton R. *Worship and Freedom: A Black American Church in Zambia.* New York: Africana Publishing Company, 1977.

Jordan, Artishia W. *The A.M.E. Church in Africa.* Privately Printed, 1960?

Payne, Daniel A. *A History of the A.M.E. Church.* Nashville: A.M.E. Sunday School Union, 1891.

Reid, Robert Henry, Jr. *Irony of Afro-American History.* A.M.E.C. Publishing, 1984.

Singleton, George A. *The Romance of African Methodism.* New York: Exposition Press, 1952.

Smith, Charles S. *A History of the A.M.E. Church.* Philadelphia: A.M.E. Book Concern, 1922.

Walker, Clarence. *A Rock in a Weary Land: The African Methodist Episcopal Church During the Civil War and Reconstruction.* Baton Rouge: Louisiana State University Press, 1982.

Wright, Charlotte C. *Beneath the Southern Cross.* New York: Exposition Press, 1955.

Wright, R.R., Jr. *Encyclopedia of African Methodism*. Philadelphia: The Book Concern of the A.M.E. Church, 1947.

BIOGRAPHICS AND AUTOBIOGRAPHICS

Allen, Richard. *The Life Experience and Gospel Labors of Rt. Rev. Richard Allen*. Nashville: Abingdon Press, 1960.

Berry, Leonidas H. *I Wouldn't Take Nothing for My Journey*. Chicago: Johnson Publishing Co., 1981.

Heard, William H. *From Slavery to the Bishopric in the A.M.E. Church*. New York: Arno Press, Reprint 1969.

Humez, Jeah M., ed. *Gifts of Power: The Writings of Rebecca Jackson*. Amherst: University of Massachusetts Press, 1981.

Lee, Jarena. *Religious Experiences and Journal of Mrs. Jarena Lee*. Philadelphia, 1849.

Payne, Daniel A. *Recollections of Seventy Years*. New York: Arno Press, Reprint 1969.

Ponton, Mungo M. *The Life and Times of Henry McNeal Turner*. Westport, Connecticut: Negro Universities Press, Reprint 1971.

Ransom, Reverdy, C. *The Pilgrimage of Harriet Ransom's Son*. Nashville: A.M.E. Sunday School Union, n.d.

Singleton, George A. *The Autobiography of George A. Singleton*. Boston: Forum Publishing Company, 1964.

Singleton, George A., ed. *The Life and Labors of Jordan Winston Early*. Nashville: A.M.E. Sunday School Union, 1894.

Smith, David, (Henderson S. Davis, editor). *Biography of Rev. David Smith of the A.M.E. Church*. Xenia, Ohio: Xenia Gazette Office, 1881.

Wesley, Charles H. *Richard Allen: Apostle of Freedom*. Washington, D.C.: Associated Publishers, 1935.

Wright, Richard R., Jr. *Eighty-Seven Years Behind the Black Curtain*. Philadelphia: Rare Book Company, 1965.

Wright, Richard R., Jr. *The Bishops of the A.M.E. Church*. Nashville: A.M.E. Sunday School Union, 1963.

ARTICLES

Andrews, Dee. "The African Methodists of Philadelphia, 1974-1802," *Pennsylvania Magazine of History and Biography*, Oct.1984, vol. CVIII, No. 4, pp. 471-486.

Dickerson, Dennis C. "Black Ecumenicism: Efforts to Establish a United Methodist Episcopal Church," *Church History*, December 1983, vol. 42, No. 4, pp. 479-491.

Dickerson, Dennis C. "William Fisher Dickerson: Northern Preacher / Southern Prelate," *Methodist History*, April 1985, vol. XXIII, No. 3, pp. 135-152.

Hall, Robert L. "The Gospel According to Radicalism: African Methodism Comes to Tallahassee AFter the Civil War," *Apalachee: Publication of the Tallahassee Historical Society,* vol. VIII, 1971-79, pp. 69-81.

Markwel, Matel. "The Rev. Daniel Coker of Sierra Leone," in David W. Wills and Richard Newman, editors, *Black Apostles at Home and Abroad.* Boston, G.K. Hall, 1982, pp. 203-210.

McBride, David. "Solomon Porter Hood, 1853-1943: Black Missionary, Educator and Minister to Liberia," *Journal of the Lancaster County Historical Society,* vol. 84, No. 1, 1980, pp. 2-9.

Miller, Floyd J. "The Father of Black Nationalism: Another Contender" (Lewis Woodson), *Civil War History,* SVII, 1971, pp. 310-320.

Page, Carol A. "Colonial Reaction to A.M.E. Missionaries in South Africa, 1898-1910," in Sylvia M. Jacobs, editor, *Black Americans and the Missionary Movement in Africa.* Westport, Connecticut: Greenwood Press, 1982, pp. 177-198.

Redkey, Edwin S. "Bishop Turner's African Dream," *Journal of American History,* September, 1967, vol. 54, No. 2, pp. 271-290.